SCIENCE AROUND THE WORLD

SCIENCE AROUND THE WORLD

Travel through Time and Space
with Fun Experiments and Projects

Shar Levine and Leslie Johnstone

Illustrations by Laurel Aiello

John Wiley & Sons, Inc.
New York • Chichester • Brisbane • Toronto • Singapore

To Christopher—a future scientist—whose idea it was
—S. L. and L. J.

As always, to Paul, Josh, Shira, and my mom—thanks
—S. L.

Also to Mark, Nicholas, and Megan
—L. J.

Acknowledgments

Our thanks to Wendy Porter for her advice and information about the Maya.
Thanks also to Dr. David Hawes and the members of the science
department at Point Grey Secondary School, Vancouver, Canada.

This text is printed on acid-free paper.

Copyright © 1996 by Shar Levine and Leslie Johnstone
Published by John Wiley & Sons, Inc.
Illustrations © 1996 by Laurel Aiello

All rights reserved. Published simultaneously in Canada.

Reproduction or translation of any part of this work beyond that permitted by section 107 or 108 of the 1976 United States Copyright Act without the permissions of the copyright owner is unlawful. Requests for permission or further information should be addressed to the Permissions Department, John Wiley & Sons, Inc.

The publisher and the author have made every reasonable effort to insure that the experiments and activities in the book are safe when conducted as instructed but assume no responsibility for any damage caused or sustained while performing the experiments or activities in this book. Parents, guardians, and/or teachers should supervise young readers who undertake the experiments and activities in this book.

Library of Congress Cataloging-in-Publication Data
Levine, Shar
    Science around the world / Shar Levine and Leslie Johnstone.
      p. cm.
    Includes index.
    ISBN 0-471-11916-4 (pbk. : alk. paper)
    1. Science—History. 2. Science—Experiments—History.
  3. Science—Miscellanea.   I. Johnstone, Leslie. II. Title.
Q125.L45 1996
509–dc20
                                                    95-44029

Printed in the United States of America
10 9 8 7 6 5 4 3 2 1

CONTENTS..........

SCIENCE AROUND THE WORLD

INTRODUCTION......................................

Travel with us to ancient times and far-away places to explore some of the world's most exciting scientific discoveries. Then return to your own backyard, where you can perform some of these same experiments yourself. Build a pyramid using the same techniques the Egyptians did. Use modern materials to make paper following a 2,000-year-old recipe. Or go fly a kite, as Mabel Bell did, to learn about aircraft design. This book will help you understand how science from different times and different places affects your everyday life.

You are not the only child in the world who studies science and math. In fact, some child halfway around the globe may be solving the same math questions that you are working on in school. After all, the language of mathematics is spoken everywhere. Today, scientists around the world can easily communicate and cooperate with each other. They provide information about their research through journals, conventions, and even computer networks.

This book will tell you about the work of great scientists from 10 different countries.

You will discover that people since the beginning of time have performed some kind of investigation of the world around them. You will learn how science from thousands of years ago is still being used today.

Each nation has something unique to offer. If you'd like to learn more about a country, scientist, or experiment featured in this book, visit your local library and read up on it.

You can also share science with children in another country. There are international science fairs and olympiads where children from around the world meet to share ideas and discoveries. By appreciating and respecting each country's scientific achievements, you will gain a better understanding of other cultures.

The most important thing is to enjoy science. Each time you perform an experiment, think about the country from which it came. Imagine another child in that country performing the same experiment in his or her own kitchen at the same time you are! You will have joined the international community of scientists.

NOTE FOR TEACHERS AND PARENTS

This book is designed to give a few fun examples of science and scientists from the countries we had space to cover. It is not intended to be an exhaustive examination of every country and its science. While there is a historical aspect to many of the experiments, we do not wish to imply that these countries are no longer engaged in scientific inquiry. Scientific research goes on today in nearly all countries of the world.

Teachers

For those of you teaching a particular science, please notice the examples here from chemistry (Mining for Crystals), physics (How Do You Like Them Apples?), biology (Orange You Glad?), astronomy (The Rocket's Red Glare), geology (Shake, Rattle, and Roll), and many other areas. And if you're teaching about the history, geography, food, or dress of a particular country, you can include activities and information about science and scientists from that country. You might even want to use the experiments and the scientists profiled as ideas for school science or history projects. Get your students to dress up as their favorite scientist and present a report on what that scientist discovered or invented. To encourage girls and boys to be more involved in science, you might wish to profile both famous women and men who were scientists.

Parents

You do not need anything special to perform most of these activities. The experiments are designed to use everyday materials. We've tried to make these experiments as safe as possible. Before allowing children to perform any of the activities, read the instructions thoroughly. Some experiments require close supervision and instruction.

The most important thing to remember is to have fun!

CHAPTER 1 EGYPT

Imagine you could travel through time and space to the banks of the Nile River in ancient Egypt. You would need to travel back in time more than 3,000 years. You would see the Nile, the longest river in Africa, being used for transportation and for irrigating crops. You might see sailing ships made of cedar wood or boats made of **papyrus**, a type of reed that grows by the river. There would be fields of wheat growing and, perhaps, some cattle grazing. Far in the distance you would see the four-sided **pyramids**, which are tombs for the **pharaohs**, or kings of Egypt.

Archaeologists, scientists who study the remains of past civilizations, have learned much about life in ancient Egypt from writings that have been discovered. The ancient Egyptians used papyrus reeds not only to build boats but also to write upon. They cut the reeds into thin pieces and formed them into flat sheets they could use like paper.

These papyruses described how Egyptians **embalmed**, or preserved, bodies to make the mummies that they then entombed, or sealed up, in the pyramids.

PYRAMID POWER

About 90 Egyptian pyramids have been found so far. These buildings, containing burial chambers, storage rooms, and passageways, were made from huge blocks of limestone. Archaeologists believe these blocks were transported along the Nile on barges and then dragged up long ramps by teams of men using ropes and wooden rollers. In this experiment you will look at the simple machines that were used in the building of the pyramids and see how they might have made the construction of these huge structures possible.

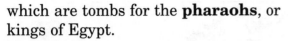

You Will Need

3 bricks, wooden blocks, or large books

a rigid piece of wood 4 to 6 inches (10 to 15 cm) wide and 3 to 4 feet (1 to 1.3 m) long

yard or meter stick

pencil and paper

3-foot (1-m) piece of string

hardcover book

spring scale or fishing scale

drinking straws

helper

What to Do

1. Stack the bricks. Place one end of the piece of wood on top of the bricks to make a ramp.

2. Use the yard or meter stick to measure the length and height of the ramp. Record this measurement.

3. Slip the piece of string through the middle of the hardcover book. Tie the string around the spine of the book so that you can lift the book up using the string.

4. Attach the spring scale to the end of the string opposite the book.

5. Using the spring scale, lift the book straight up. Record the weight showing on the scale. This shows the amount of **force** (a push or pull) you need to use to pull the book straight up.

6. Using the spring scale, pull the book smoothly up the ramp. Note the weight reading of the spring scale.

scale

string

book

ANCIENT EGYPT

7. Have a helper place drinking straws under the book as you pull it up the ramp. Now what weight does the scale read?

What Happened

The ramp is a type of simple machine called an **inclined plane** (a sloped surface that allows you to raise objects more easily). When you lifted the book straight up, you needed to use more force than when you lifted it using the ramp. When your helper added the straws, you could lift the book using even less force. This is because the straws reduced the **friction** (a force that resists motion when one surface slides over another) caused by the book rubbing against the wood. The drinking straws reduced the friction because only a small amount of the straws' surface touched the ramp or the book at any one time.

Comparing the length of the ramp to its height tells you how easy it will be to pull an object up the ramp. If the length of the ramp is twice the height, you can lift twice as much weight using the same amount of force. The ratio of length divided by height is referred to as **mechanical advantage**. A ramp with a large mechanical advantage will allow you to move a very heavy object with much less force. The blocks of limestone required to build the pyramids each weighed about two tons. The ramps used to move them needed to have a very large mechanical advantage.

AMAZING SCIENCE

The most well-known pyramid still standing is the Great Pyramid of Khufu. Scientists estimate that it took 100,000 men to build the Great Pyramid. It contains more than 2.3 million limestone blocks, each weighing 2.5 tons. It took 20 years to build and is 480 feet (146 m) high. That's almost 200 feet (61 m) taller than the Statue of Liberty. At the time the pyramid was built it was the tallest structure in the world. Today, the CN Tower in Toronto, Ontario, Canada, at 1,815 feet (553 m) is the tallest freestanding structure in the world.

Some people think that pyramids and objects shaped like pyramids have special powers. They believe that pyramids can keep food fresher, improve the taste of wine, sharpen razor blades, and make meat more tender. They also think that if a plant is placed under a pyramid-shaped frame, it will grow faster. This belief, most popular during the 1970s, came from the idea that the Egyptian pyramids had magical powers. Careful scientific research has found no support for these claims. You might want to try your own experiments to test this theory.

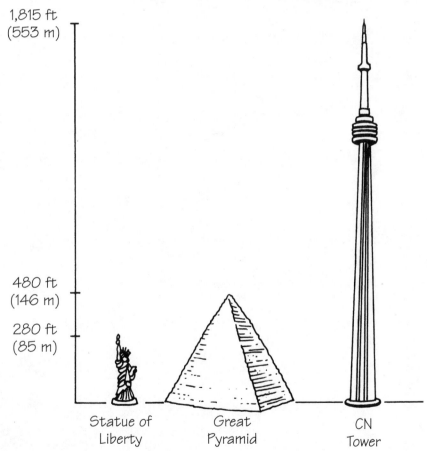

1,815 ft
(553 m)

480 ft
(146 m)

280 ft
(85 m)

Statue of
Liberty

Great
Pyramid

CN
Tower

CHAPTER 2 CHINA

There have been many amazing inventions and scientific discoveries in China during the thousands of years of its civilization. Some things we still use every day were invented long ago in China. The Chinese invented fireworks around the sixth century A.D. and gunpowder as early as 1200. Other familiar Chinese inventions include matches, axes, porcelain, clocks, and even the paper you write on.

Many great scientists have come from China, including Zhang Heng, whose work is profiled at the end of this chapter. In addition to measuring earthquakes, Zhang Heng also correctly believed that the moon was lit by the sun and that eclipses were caused by the earth's shadow. In the fifth century A.D. the Chinese mathematician and astronomer Zu Chonzhi estimated the number *pi* so accurately that it took over 1,000 years before a more precise measurement was made.

Great Wall (Paper)

Many people think the Egyptians invented the first paper. This is not correct. Although the word *paper* comes from the Egyptian word *papyrus,* papyrus sheets were not true paper. By definition, paper must be made from **fibers** (thin, threadlike pieces of plant or animal materials), which are beaten with water, then drained through a screen. In China, around 2,000 years ago, a man named Ts'ai Lun was the first person to create a piece of paper. Although Ts'ai Lun used tree bark, rope, pieces of cloth, and other fibrous materials to make his paper, you can make your own paper using lint from your dryer.

You Will Need

any used white paper, such as computer paper, or envelopes with the plastic window removed

lint from your dryer

measuring cup

blender

water

grass, leaves, or flower petals (optional)

roasting pan or other large, flat container

food coloring (optional)

8-by-11-inch (20-by-28-cm) fine plastic
    screen—available from any hardware store

newspapers or towels

sponge

adult helper

What to Do

1. Rip the paper into small bits. Make
sure you remove any plastic or
metal pieces from the paper.

2. Place ½ cup (125 ml) of lint and
1 cup (250 ml) of finely shredded
paper into the blender.

water
(2 cups, or
500 ml)

shredded
paper

dryer lint

flower petals,
grass, and leaves

3. Add about 2 cups (500 ml) of water
to the blender. (If you have a small
blender, add less water and paper.)
If you wish, you can add a handful
of petals, grass, or leaves to the
mixture to give the paper a more
interesting appearance.

4. Have an adult "pulse" the mixture
by turning the blender off and on.
Blend the mixture until it is the
texture of cooked oatmeal. Add
more water to the blender if the
blades are not turning smoothly.

5. Pour the mixture into the roasting
pan and add another 2 to 3 cups
(500 to 750 ml) of water.

6. Stir the mixture with your hands to
mix it evenly. If you wish, you can
add several drops of food coloring at
this point to make colored paper.

7. Hold the screen firmly with both
hands and dip below the surface of
the mixture. Allow the screen to be
covered with the pulp.

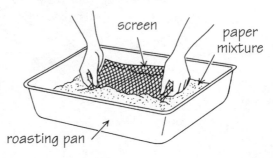

screen

paper
mixture

roasting pan

8. Lift the screen out of the roasting pan, using a steady motion. Hold the screen over the roasting pan for several seconds so the water drips back into the pan.

9. Place the screen, wet paper side up, onto several pieces of newspaper. Cover this with more newspaper and use the sponge to soak up the excess water.

10. Slowly remove the top sheets of newspaper.

11. Turn the screen upside down onto a clean, dry piece of paper. Gently peel back the screen to reveal the wet piece of homemade paper. Allow to dry in a warm spot.

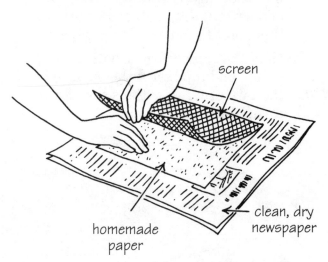

screen

homemade paper

clean, dry newspaper

What Happened

All paper is made up of some kind of fiber. Fibers can be found in plants and even in animal fur. To be used in paper-making, fibers must be able to soak up water. The uneven edges of the fibers stick together as the water is drained from them.

If you hold an expensive piece of paper up to the light, you may see a marking telling you the "rag" content of the paper. Rag content means the paper was made using some cotton or linen fibers. Today, most paper is made using wood fiber.

Used paper can be broken up and made into new paper, just as you did in the experiment. This process gives you *recycled* paper. Some new fibers must be added each time you recycle paper, or the paper will be too weak to use.

SANDS OF TIME

The hourglass, or sand timer, was first invented by the ancient Chinese. Scientists have been unable to establish when the first hourglass was made, but the first mention of its use was in about the third century B.C. The Chinese used the **clepsydra**, or water clock, as far back as the sixth century B.C., and they also used some of the first mechanical clocks. It's easy to build your own sand clock—try it and see.

You Will Need

3 identical clear plastic soda bottles—the 16-ounce (500-ml) size is the best

dishwashing liquid

scissors

2-inch (5-cm) piece of plastic tubing, with an inside diameter of 1 inch (2.5 cm)—available at most hardware or aquarium supply stores

2-cup (500-ml) measuring cup

fine sand

1-inch (2.5-cm) metal washer

masking tape

watch with a second hand

felt markers

adult helper

What to Do

1. Peel the labels from two of the bottles, then soak the bottles in warm, soapy water to remove the glue.

2. Rinse the bottles until all the soap is removed and allow them to dry completely. (This is very important! If the bottles are damp inside, the sand will stick to the plastic.)

3. Have the adult cut the top third off the last plastic bottle. This will be your funnel.

4. Fit the plastic tubing *over* the mouth of one of the bottles. It is best to do this before you fill the bottle with sand, just in case you drop the bottle while trying to do this!

5. Fill the measuring cup with 2 cups (500 ml) of fine sand.

6. Insert the small opening of the funnel in the plastic tubing and pour the sand into the funnel.

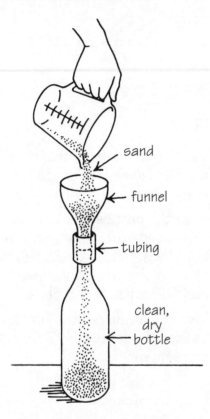

sand

funnel

tubing

clean,
dry
bottle

7. When the sand has flowed into the bottle, remove the funnel and place the washer into the tubing. Keep pressing the washer down until it rests on the lip of the bottle. The hole in the washer should be over the opening of the bottle.

8. Turn the second bottle upside down and insert the opening into the plastic tubing. Have your helper hold the bottom bottle while you push down on the top bottle to make a complete connection.

9. Place a piece of masking tape down the side of each bottle.

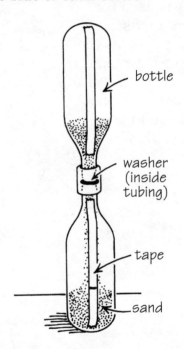

bottle

washer
(inside
tubing)

tape

sand

10. Turn the bottle upside down. Time for exactly 1 minute as the sand flows down. Draw a line on the masking tape at the spot the sand reaches after 1 minute.

11. Take the top bottle off and remove all the sand over the 1-minute line.

12. Replace the top bottle as before. You now have your own 1-minute timer.

13. Once you have discovered how much sand is needed for a 1-minute timer, experiment to see if half that amount of sand will give you a 30-second timer. Will twice as much give you a 2-minute timer?

What Happened

The amount of sand you had to use depended on the diameter of the opening of the bottle and the size of the tubing. The sand traveled from one bottle to the other because of gravity. Gravity always pulls at the same rate, so it always takes the same amount of time for the sand to fall. It should take about twice as much time for twice the sand to flow through the opening between the bottles. If the sand gets damp or packed together, it may not flow freely. If this happens, open the timer up and allow the sand to dry.

AMAZING SCIENTIST

Zhang Heng was a Chinese scientist who lived around A.D. 78–139. Zhang invented a device that recorded the strength and location of earthquakes. His device was a metal jar with a cover. Around the sides of the jar were eight dragon heads, each holding a ball. Inside the jar was a heavy weight hanging from a wire. During an earthquake the weight would swing, knocking a ball from a dragon's mouth into the mouth of a metal toad located below it.

The ball striking the metal toad made a very loud noise. This showed that an earthquake had occurred. The number of balls that fell indicated the strength of the earthquake. Depending on which ball (or balls) fell, Zhang Heng could also tell the direction in which the earthquake took place. This early **seismograph** (a device used to detect and measure earthquakes) first recorded a quake in A.D. 132.

CHAPTER 3 MEXICO

The ancient Maya lived in part of what is now Mexico from about A.D. 250 to A.D. 900. Their civilization stretched from southern Mexico to Belize, Guatemala, and Honduras. The Maya built huge pyramids, similar to those of the Egyptians, and temples in which they worshiped their many gods.

The ancient Maya civilization was very advanced. Nineteen hundred years ago, the Maya created calendars and other astronomical measuring systems, as well as a complicated written language of **hieroglyphs** (a way of writing that uses pictures to represent a word, sound, or syllable).

HANGING BY A THREAD

The Maya have long been famous for their buildings, calendars, pottery, art, and language. We can now add bridge building to this list. Recently, archaeologists and **engineers** (scientists who apply science and technology to solve practical problems) have discovered the remains of the world's earliest **suspension bridge** (a bridge that is held up by cables). Using computers, videotapes, and pictures taken from a plane, the researchers found the bridge, which was located across the Usumacinta River in Yaxchilán, Mexico. This ancient bridge was made from trees, twined plant materials, and masonry. It's hard to believe that the Maya could have built a bridge 590 feet (180 m) long over 1,200 years ago! Let's see how they did it.

You Will Need

a piece of heavy cardboard 2 feet by 4 feet (60 cm by 120 cm)

4 bricks or wooden blocks

yard or meter stick

large ball of strong string

duct tape or other heavy tape

scissors

a long piece of lightweight cardboard 6 inches by 5 feet (15 cm by 150 cm)

What to Do

1. Place the heavy piece of cardboard on a firm surface. This is the base for your bridge.

2. Place the 4 bricks on end on top of the cardboard so that they form the corners of a rectangle 7 inches (17.5 cm) wide and 2 feet (60 cm) long. These are your **towers**.

3. Tape one end of the string to one 2-foot (60-cm) edge of the cardboard in line with one of the bricks. This is the **anchor**. Drape the string over the top of the brick, straight across the space between the bricks, and over the opposite brick. Leave enough string so that it hangs down between the bricks about 3 inches (7.5 cm). Tape the loose end of the string to the opposite side of the 2-foot (60-cm) edge of cardboard. This will form

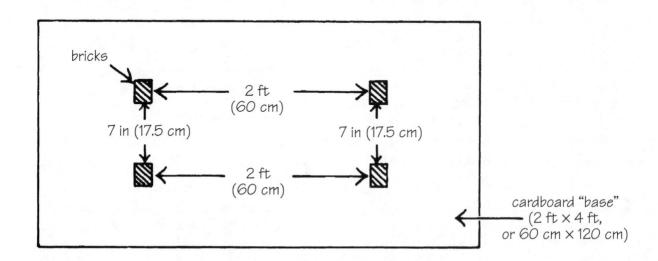

bricks

2 ft (60 cm)

7 in (17.5 cm)   7 in (17.5 cm)

2 ft (60 cm)

cardboard "base" (2 ft × 4 ft, or 60 cm × 120 cm)

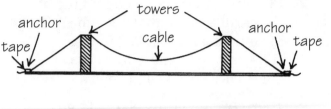

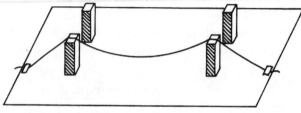

the other anchor. Cut the string from the ball. The length of string hanging between the bricks is called the **cable**.

4. Do the same thing on the other side of the bridge, using the other two bricks. Make sure this string hangs down the same distance as the first cable. You now have two cables.

5. Carefully slide the long piece of lightweight cardboard so it stretches the length of the bridge and lies on the other piece of cardboard between the bricks. This will be the **platform**, or roadway, for your bridge.

6. Cut six 12-inch (30-cm) pieces of string. Tie one end of one piece of string every 4 inches (10 cm) along

one of the cables. These are your **suspenders**.

7. Slide each of the suspenders under the long piece of lightweight cardboard. Now comes the tricky part. Tie the free end of each of the suspenders to the other cable. The suspenders closest to the towers should be longer than those in the middle of the bridge. In the middle of the bridge the platform should be suspended about 3 inches (7.5 cm) above the cardboard base. Trim the excess string from the suspenders.

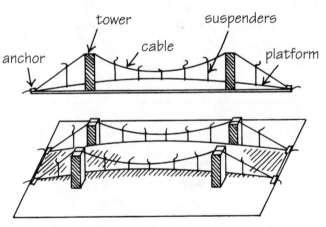

8. Now that your platform is hung, gently bend the ends so that they touch the cardboard base. Tape the ends to the base. You now have a road that goes across a suspended bridge.

What Happened

You have created a suspension bridge. The suspenders take the weight of the platform or road up to the cables. The cables then carry this weight to the towers and the anchors. The weight of the platform pulls upward on the anchors and downward on the towers. The towers are strong rigid structures, like your bricks, so they can support a lot of weight. The anchors need to be well secured to a firm object (usually land), like your cardboard base, so that they don't pull loose. Suspension bridges use much less material than traditional bridges and can span large distances.

Did You Know?

○ When it is completed, the longest suspension bridge in the world will be the Messina Bridge in Italy. This bridge will join Calabria (the "toe" of Italy) and the island of Sicily. Its **span** (the distance between towers) will be 10,892 feet (3,320 m).

AMAZING SCIENCE

The ancient Maya invented a complicated calendar that repeated every 52 years. They gave each day within the calendar a different set of names. This meant that a Maya child's birthday would be called by a different day, week, and month name each year. Although this may seem confusing, the Maya calendar was very accurate. In fact, it is thought to be more accurate than the one we use now.

Using this calendar, the Maya could predict practical things, such as the

beginning of the rainy season for planting, or events far in the future, such as when planets would appear in the night sky. The calendar also listed when eclipses of the sun and moon would occur. With such a complicated system, people relied on **shamans** (tribal healers or religious leaders) to tell them what day it was. The shaman would also give them advice as to what days were "good" or lucky.

Did You Know?

○ The Maya used mathematics to calculate huge spans of time. One rare Maya inscription calculates a span of more than 40 octillion years (that's 40 followed by 27 zeros). That number is so large that it is billions of times larger than scientists have calculated for the age of the universe!

CHAPTER 4 GERMANY

What do zeppelins, Fahrenheit thermometers, diesel engines, Bunsen burners, and Mercedes-Benz automobiles have in common? They are all named after German scientists! Germany has been an important center for scientific learning since the sixteenth century. Around 1447, a goldsmith named Johannes Gutenberg invented a new type of printing press that allowed people to print many copies of their ideas. Because of Gutenberg's invention, scientific ideas and theories soon spread throughout the world. This information revolution led to a time of great scientific discovery.

Other scientific breakthroughs from Germany include liquid fuel rockets, X rays, diesel engines, mercury thermometers, spectroscopes, and automobiles. Try an experiment that explains an interesting scientific discovery made in Germany—the effect of air pressure.

WILD HORSES COULDN'T TEAR ME AWAY

This experiment—the first to show the strength of air pressure—was designed in 1654 by Otto von Guericke, the mayor of Magdeburg, Germany. He performed it before Emperor Ferdinand III, and you can imagine the look of surprise on the Emperor's face as he watched two teams of eight horses each trying to pull apart two empty metal bowls. Von Guericke had placed the bowls together to form a hollow ball, then had the air between them pumped

out to form a **vacuum** (a space that contains no air). As soon as some air was allowed to go back in, the bowls came apart easily.

See if you can impress your friends as much as von Guericke wowed his famous visitors.

You Will Need

2 clean plungers (the kind used to unplug toilets—available at any hardware store)

sink

water

paper clip

1-foot (30-cm) piece of string

small suction cup

flattopped wooden or metal stool

helper

What to Do

Experiment 1

1. Make sure the plungers are clean before you try this experiment. You might want to rinse them in warm water before you start.

2. Wet the rubber rim of both plungers in water.

3. Have your helper hold one of the plungers by the handle, so the rubber suction end is pointing away from his or her body and toward you.

4. Press your end of the suction part of the other plunger onto your helper's plunger. Push them together slightly to remove some of the air. The two should now form a tight seal.

5. Both you and your helper should try to separate the plungers by pulling with all your might.

6. If you cannot separate the plungers by pulling, slip a paper clip between the rims of the plungers to let a little bit of air in, then try pulling. Did this make a difference?

Experiment 2

1. Tie the string to the stem end of a suction cup.

2. Lightly wet the inside of the suction cup and stick it to the center of the stool's top.

3. Use the string to lift up the suction cup Does the suction cup lift the chair, too?

4. Try it again, this time without wetting the suction cup. Did this make a difference?

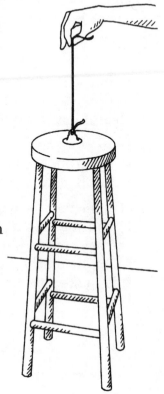

What Happened

In the first experiment, the plungers stuck together and could not be pulled apart until you placed the paper clip between the rims. This is because of the strength of the vacuum inside the plungers. You created this vacuum when you removed some of the air between the plungers by pushing them together. Because there was so little air inside the plungers, the **air pressure** (the force that air places on a certain area) outside the plungers was greater than the air pressure inside. Once you allowed air to enter the space by using the paper clip, you were able to pull the plungers apart because the air pressure became equal inside and outside the plungers.

A similar thing happened with the suction cup. Pushing the suction cup down onto the stool removed the air from under the cup. The vacuum created allowed you to lift the stool. Wetting the suction cup made it easier to stick it to the surface of the chair.

Did You Know?

○ Plungers clear blocked drains by sealing the opening to the drain and allowing you to change the amount of pressure going into the drain. When you push down, you increase the pressure, and when you pull up, you decrease the pressure. This usually loosens the material causing the blockage and allows the drain to clear.

AMAZING SCIENTIST

Earlier in this book we wrote about what might happen if you could travel back in time. One famous German-born scientist, Albert Einstein, said that if you could travel quickly enough, time would slow down. Some scientists think that if it were possible to go fast enough, you might even make time go backward. Science fiction writers have used this idea to suggest that time machines would work if they could travel faster than the speed of light. Since light travels about 186,000 miles per second (300,000 km per second), this would have to be a very fast machine!

ARCTIC OCEAN

UNITED KINGDOM

ATLANTIC OCEAN

PACIFIC OCEAN

INDIAN OCEAN

PACIFIC OCEAN

CHAPTER 5 UNITED KINGDOM

Do you belong to a club or group like Guides or Scouts? Scientists also belong to groups. They get together to discuss their ideas and research. One of the world's best-known groups was started in 1662 when a number of British scientists formed the Royal Society, which still exists today. The Royal Society encourages the work of scientists and engineers, prints the results of their research, and holds conferences for the scientists to discuss their work. Their members have included the most important scientists in England. One of their first presidents was Sir Isaac Newton, whose ideas form the basis of our next experiment.

How Do You Like Them Apples?

Sir Isaac Newton was a famous British scientist who lived from 1642 to 1727. He is considered to be one of the greatest scientists who ever lived. He is probably most famous for his discovery of the law of **gravity** (the force that pulls objects toward other large objects, such as the earth). Newton is said to have been inspired to think about gravity when he observed an apple falling from an apple tree. He used his theories about gravity to estimate the **mass** (the amount of material something contains) of the earth and the masses of other known planets. To help him observe the planets, Newton built a new kind of telescope.

Newton also wrote laws explaining the way objects move. These laws helped other scientists explain the way the planets move around the sun. Here is an experiment to test one of Newton's laws of motion.

You Will Need

drinking glass

index card or piece of light cardboard

a marble

an audience

What to Do

1. Place the glass on a table and cover the opening with the index card.

2. Carefully place the marble on top of the index card so that it rests in the center of the card.

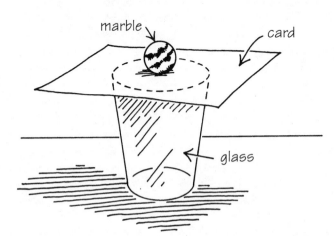

marble

card

glass

3. Use your forefinger and thumb in a flicking motion to snap the card away from the top of the glass. Practice this until you can get the marble to fall into the glass every time.

4. Now try it for an audience.

What Happened

The index card moved sideways, but the marble didn't. The marble moved down when gravity pulled it into the glass. Newton discovered that objects that are not moving stay in one place, unless a force pushes or pulls on them, while objects that are moving keep moving in the same direction. This property is called **inertia.** Objects that have large masses have more inertia. Since the mass of the marble was large compared with the mass of the index card, the marble stayed in place unless you hit it, while the card moved.

If you were to move the card away slowly, the marble would move with it and roll off the card onto the table. This is because friction has a greater effect on objects that are moving slowly than on objects that are moving quickly. This effect explains how magicians can pull a tablecloth out from under a complete table setting without breaking anything. (Don't try this last trick at home—unless you have very understanding parents and unbreakable dishes!)

MINING FOR CRYSTALS

Dorothy Hodgkin is a famous modern British scientist. In 1964 she won a Nobel Prize in chemistry for her work with **crystals** (regularly shaped repeating units of chemicals). Hodgkin used crystals to discover the structure of molecules such as **penicillin** (a drug used to cure infections) and vitamin B_{12}. Some chemicals have crystals with very special shapes that grow in interesting ways. Try this experiment to grow some crystals of your own.

You Will Need

6 charcoal briquettes (plain kind, with no lighter fluid)

thick paper bag

hammer

⅓ cup (75 ml) laundry bluing

water

measuring cup

2 old plastic containers—larger than 2 cups (500 ml)

measuring spoon

⅓ cup (75 ml) of one of the following: salt, borax, or Epsom salts

⅓ cup (75 ml) water

1 tablespoon (15 ml) ammonia

food coloring

What to Do

Perform this experiment close to an open window or in a well-ventilated room.

1. Put the charcoal in a bag and use a hammer to break the briquettes into pieces.

2. If you are using powdered laundry bluing, mix the powder with an equal amount of water. If the laundry bluing is liquid, add about 2 tablespoons (30 ml) of water to it.

3. Place all of the ingredients except the food coloring and the charcoal into a plastic container and mix.

4. Place the charcoal bits into the other plastic container and pour the liquid mixture over the coal. Add a drop of food coloring to the top of the coals. Put the container somewhere safe, where it can sit undisturbed for a day.

5. Do not move the container, as the crystals are delicate. Watch throughout the day as the crystals form.

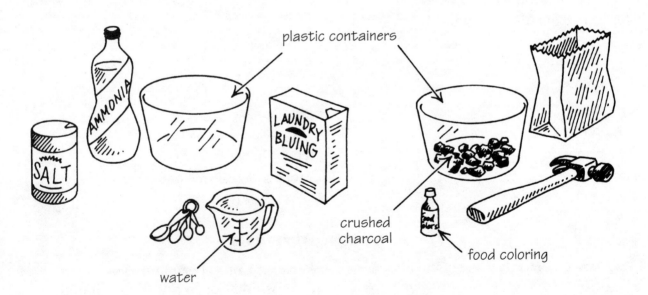

plastic containers

SALT

AMMONIA

LAUNDRY BLUING

water

crushed charcoal

food coloring

What Happened

After a little while crystals began to form on the surface of the charcoal. The salt, borax, or Epsom salts were dissolved in the water. The briquettes absorbed some of the water and acted as a surface to allow the crystals to form. The bluing, ammonia, and salt mixed together to form a crystal. As the water was absorbed by the charcoal, small particles of the salts came out of the water and **bonded** (joined together) in a repeating pattern.

When millions of these small particles are joined together, they form the crystal shapes that you see. Each type of chemical that forms a crystal has its own characteristic crystal shape. For example, Epsom salts form long, needle-shaped crystals, while table salt forms crystals in the shape of a cube.

AMAZING SCIENCE

DNA (deoxyribonucleic acid) is the chemical that provides the instructions for how living things grow and develop. Every living thing has its own particular structure of DNA. The basic shape of the DNA **molecule** (a small particle made up of two or more atoms) was discovered in 1953 by British scientists Francis Crick and Maurice Wilkins and American scientist James Watson. They were able to tell what shape it had because it could be made into a crystal and measured using the same techniques Dorothy Hodgkin used. The work of another British scientist, Rosalind Franklin, made it possible for the structure of DNA to be discovered.

ARCTIC OCEAN

CANADA

ATLANTIC OCEAN

PACIFIC OCEAN

INDIAN OCEAN

PACIFIC OCEAN

CHAPTER 6 CANADA

Canadian scientists have made many discoveries and advances that affect our lives today. For example, it was a Canadian engineer, Sir Sandford Fleming, who created the system of standard time, which divides the world into 24 time zones. Imagine how confusing life would be if you didn't know what time it was in another part of the world, or even in the next state or province.

Canadian scientist Sir Frederick Banting was one of the discoverers of **insulin,** the drug that helps control diabetes.

Several Canadians have also won science's greatest award, the Nobel Prize. Gerhard Hurtzberg and John Polanyi each won the Nobel Prize for their work in chemistry, and Michael Smith won one for his work with DNA.

Oil's Well That Ends Well

Dr. Abraham Gesner was a Canadian scientist whose research, designs, and experiments contributed to the creation of the modern oil and gas industry. In the process, he also helped save whales.

In the early 1800s, Gesner worked as a government **geologist** (a scientist who studies rocks and minerals) for the province of Nova Scotia. He looked for ways that different minerals could be used as fuel. At that time, there were no electric lightbulbs; people had only lamps that burned thick oil. When any of these oils burned, they created a dense, black smoke with a terrible smell. Oil from **lard** (solid fat from animals), fish, and seeds was used in these lamps, but most people preferred oil from whales because it gave off the brightest light. They also used whale oil to keep machine parts running smoothly. By 1850, whales had been hunted to the point that many species were rare and some even **extinct** (no living examples left).

Gesner created a way to manufacture **kerosene** (a liquid fuel made from coal). This new fuel not only could be used as a lamp oil, but it also took the place of the whale oil used on machinery. It gave off a bright light when burned and much less smoke than the oils. Gesner designed a factory in New York to **refine** (take a material from its natural state and change it into another, more usable, form) oil, asphalt, and coal. Here's an experiment comparing the way different oils burn.

You Will Need

cotton cord or commercial wick (available from craft stores)

ruler

scissors

small aluminum foil tart cups

clear tape

cookie sheet

different kinds of food oil

   olive oil

   peanut oil

   vegetable oil

   lard or other animal fat

spoon

paper and pencil

matches

watch with a second hand

adult helper

Warning: Do not use any kind of liquid fuel. Use only the food oils listed. This experiment must be done with adult supervision.

What to Do

1. For each kind of oil you are using, cut a 5-inch (12.5-cm) length of cord or wick.

2. Tape one end of each cord to the bottom of each tart cup and drape the other end over the rim of the tart cup. Place the tart cups on a cookie sheet.

3. Fill each tart cup about halfway with a different kind of oil. (You might have to spoon in the lard.) Make sure the wicks are still taped to the bottom of each cup. Use tape and a small piece of paper to label the tart cups with the different kinds of oil.

4. Have an adult helper light each wick. Record the length of time it

takes each oil to burn to the bottom of the tart cup. Record your observations on a chart. **Warning:** Be sure not to try to blow out the flame, as the oil could spatter. Instead, cover with a pot lid and allow the flame to go out if necessary.

What Happened

Different kinds of oil burn at different rates. This is because the oils contain chemicals with slightly different structures. The oil burns because of a chemical reaction between the oxygen in the

Type of oil	Length of time to burn	Observation (smell, smoke, etc.)

air and the chemicals that make up the oil. The flame changes the oil and oxygen from the air into carbon dioxide and water.

Carbon dioxide is an invisible gas—the same kind of gas you breathe out when you exhale. You don't see the water because it is so hot that it stays in the flame as water vapor. Black smoke is caused by carbon from the oil that didn't react with oxygen. The smell is caused by other chemicals that are present in the oil in small amounts.

Did You Know?

○ Kerosene lamps have an adjustable wick that you can use to control the amount of light the lamp gives off. You can slowly raise or lower the wick so that different amounts of it burn. The more of the wick that is burning, the brighter the light. Kerosene lamps usually have a glass chimney, which increases the amount of air surrounding the wick. This additional oxygen also causes a brighter flame.

Go Fly a Kite

Mabel Bell was a pioneer in **aviation** (the study of flight), but you might be more familiar with the work of her husband, Alexander Graham Bell, the inventor of the telephone. Her father was also well known as one of the founders of *National Geographic* magazine!

In 1907, Mrs. Bell started the Aerial Experiment Association (AEA) at the family home in Baddeck, Nova Scotia, Canada. She and her husband gathered together some of the greatest scientists and engineers of the early twentieth century to experiment with flight. Mrs. Bell hired what was to be the first research group to design airplanes. She was an active participant in much of the work done by this group and frequently helped them conduct experiments.

In 1903, Orville and Wilbur Wright flew a plane a distance of 120 feet (36.5 m) at Kitty Hawk, North Carolina, but it was the AEA that won the *Scientific American* trophy for the first flight. On July 4, 1908, the AEA's *June Bug* was the first "heavier than air" machine to fly 1 kilometer (0.6 mi) under test conditions.

Here's an experiment based on some of the early work of Mabel Bell and her husband, Alexander.

You Will Need

2 kites of the same size and shape (store-bought or homemade)

kite string

spring scale or fishing scale

helper

Warning: Always fly kites in open spaces, away from electrical wires, pylons, and roads.

What to Do

1. Make the kites following the directions on the package.

2. Take the kites to a safe and open space to fly. Attach the kite string to one of the kites.

3. Launch the kite so that it is flying about 50 feet (15 m) above the ground.

4. Tie a loop in the string and attach the spring scale to the loop. Measure the force with which the kite pulls on the string.

5. Have your helper hold the kite's string.

6. Launch the second kite to the same height. Tie a loop in the string of the second kite.

7. Attach the spring scale to the loop of the second kite's string, but do not remove it from the first kite's string. The scale should be measuring the force exerted by both of the kites at the same time.

8. Hold the kite strings and remove the spring scale before reeling in your kites.

What Happened

The kites pulled on the spring scale with a certain amount of force, depending on the force of the wind. The two kites pulled with about twice as much force as the single kite. Kites fly best when they are hit by the wind at the right angle. The forces of the wind lifting up and gravity pushing down determined the correct angle for the kites to approach the wind.

The Bells used their observations of kites to help them design better wings for their aircraft.

Did You Know?

○ Alexander Graham Bell thought that a flying machine designed like a series of small kites would be able to hold a person in the air. He used a special shape known as a **tetrahedron** to help build the lightweight, kitelike wings of his craft. Today, people glide through the air on kitelike hang gliders.

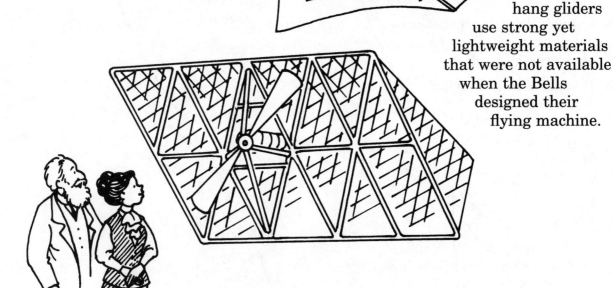

These hang gliders use strong yet lightweight materials that were not available when the Bells designed their flying machine.

○ Here's a way to test one of Bell's theories and play a trick on your friends and family. Give your friend 6 identical toothpicks. Ask your friend to use the toothpicks to make 4 triangles of the same size and shape. The toothpicks can't be broken, overlapped, or placed on top of one another. It's hard to figure out!

Solution: Place 3 of the toothpicks on a table and join them together to make a triangle. Take the remaining toothpicks and place them upright inside the first triangle to form a pyramid-shaped structure. This shape is called a tetrahedron.

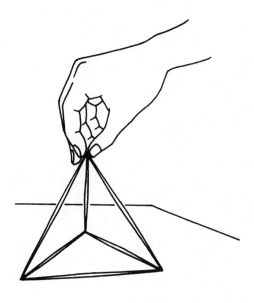

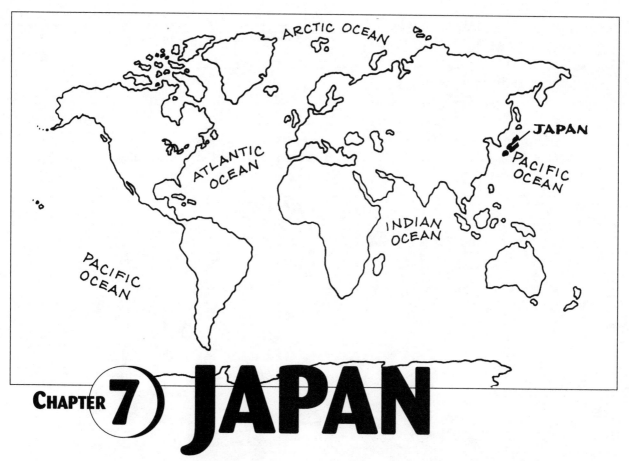

CHAPTER 7 JAPAN

A **tsunami** is a large ocean wave caused by an earthquake or underwater volcano. These waves can be up to 100 miles (160 km) long and travel up to 450 miles (725 km) per hour. While these waves are only about 1 to 2 feet (30 to 60 cm) high at sea, they can grow to be over 50 feet (15 m) high when they strike the shore. Tsunamis are so powerful they can destroy entire towns.

Because of all the geologic activity in the area, Japan has been struck by many tsunamis. Understandably, Japanese scientists have been very interested in geology. They have had great success in that area, especially in the study of earthquakes. Our next experiment will show us something of what they have learned.

SHAKE, RATTLE, AND ROLL

On January 17, 1995, a terrible earthquake struck Kobe, Japan. Over 5,000 people were killed and thousands of others injured during this severe quake. This was not the first earthquake to hit Japan. In fact, the Japanese had been preparing for the possibility for many

years. Earthquakes or other **seismic** (movement related to earthquakes) activities occur frequently in Japan. It is estimated there is some kind of seismic activity there at least three times each day.

The country is located where two **tectonic plates** (huge pieces of the earth's surface) meet. The grinding of these plates as they move against each other causes great pressure in the earth. The slipping movement of the plates to ease this pressure is what causes an earthquake.

In 1923, the Japanese designed a "shaking table" to test how buildings would stand up during an earthquake. Today, computers are used to test the stability of buildings, roads, and bridges. You can make a homemade earthquake table to give you an idea of how architects design earthquake-safe buildings.

You Will Need

a sturdy card table with four legs

a roll of wax paper

tape

balloons

building blocks, cards, and/or books

4 friends

What to Do

1. Cut a piece of wax paper long enough to stretch along all four sides of the tabletop. Tape the wax paper to make a collar around the top of the table.

2. Blow up the balloons and tie them closed.

3. Have your friends hold the table upside down so that the wax paper collar just touches the ground.

4. Put the balloons inside the wax paper collar under the table until the collar is full of balloons.

collar

table

5. Make sure your friends are holding the four legs of the table. Carefully stand in the center of the table. How does it feel? Have a friend help you on and off the table.

6. Use the blocks, cards, or books to try building small structures on the table.

7. Shake the table to simulate an earthquake. Which shapes stay standing after being shaken on your earthquake simulator?

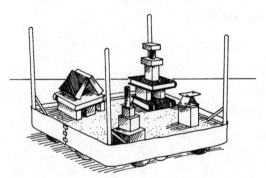

What Happened

The balloons underneath the table made it unstable, so the table moved around when you stood on it. This movement felt like the movement of the ground in an earthquake.

The amount of energy given off in an earthquake can be measured by a scale called the Richter scale. American geologist Charles Francis Richter invented the scale because he grew tired of people asking him to compare the size of quakes. The Richter scale gives numbers to the intensity of an earthquake. Each number represents an increase of 10 times the energy of the previous number. The values given for an earthquake are calculated from measurements made using seismographs (devices used to detect, measure, and record earthquakes). An earthquake measuring 3 on the Richter scale would be felt by some people.

An earthquake 10 times as strong—of magnitude 4—would be felt by most people and would cause some damage to buildings. Earthquakes of magnitude 8 and above result in major damage to any buildings in the area and often loss of lives. Most geologists nowadays use a newer scale called the moment-magnitude scale. Its readings are calculated from measurements made of earth movement.

Did You Know?

○ The safest place to be in an earthquake is in a doorway or under a table because they give the best protection.

○ Major earthquakes are often followed by a series of smaller quakes known as "aftershocks," so after an earthquake, it is a good idea to stay somewhere safe.

○ In Kobe, many buildings, roads, and railway tracks that were supposed to have been "earthquake proof," in fact, were not. Scientists from around the world are now studying the ruins to determine why the structures crumbled and how improvements can be made.

FLIP-FLOPS

Motonori Matuyama, the son of a Zen abbot, was a Japanese geologist who made an "earthshattering" discovery. Basalts, a type of volcanic rock, are magnetic. Matuyama noticed that the magnetism of the basalt rocks in different areas pointed in different directions. The pattern formed is called the **magnetic field** (the lines of force around something that is magnetic).

Matuyama used these observations to conclude that the earth's magnetic field had changed direction. This means that at some time in the past the North Pole would actually have been the South Pole. The most recent time of reversal is known as the *Matuyama reversed epoch*. As a result of his work, scientists now believe the earth's magnetic poles have reversed a number of times. Perform the following experiment to see a magnetic field.

You Will Need

2 bar magnets

8½-by-11-inch (20-by-28-cm) piece of paper

iron filings (available at toy and science stores)

notepad and pencil

What to Do

1. Place one of the bar magnets *under* the paper so that it is in the middle of the sheet.

2. Sprinkle about 2 tablespoons (30 ml) of iron filings on the top of the piece of paper.

3. Draw a picture to show the shape of iron filings around the magnet.

4. Carefully lift the paper off the magnet and place it aside. Place the second magnet about 1 inch (2.5 cm) from the first magnet, so that the opposite poles are facing each other. Do not place the magnets so close to each other that they become joined by the attraction. Put the paper with the iron filings back on top of the magnets. Draw a picture to show the shape the filings make.

5. Remove the paper with the filings and turn one of the magnets around so that two like poles now face each other. Put the paper with the filings back over the magnet. Draw a picture to show the new shape.

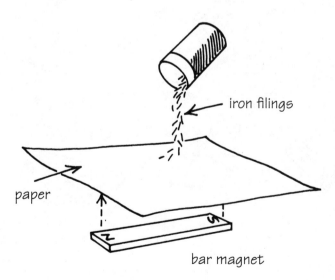

iron filings

paper

bar magnet

What Happened

In each of the experiments, the iron filings formed a distinct pattern. The iron in the filings is attracted to the magnet. Most of the filings gathered near the ends of the magnets. This is because the magnetic field is strongest there. All of the iron filings would travel to the ends of the magnet if it weren't for friction, which holds some of them back.

The farther away from the poles the filings are, the less the amount of magnetic force acting on them. When the forces of friction and magnetism balance, the filings stop moving.

AMAZING SCIENCE

○ The largest magnet in the world is . . . the world! The earth is a huge magnet. Today, the North magnetic pole is located in the sea north of Canada, while the South magnetic pole is located somewhere in Antarctica. If we could visit the earth in hundreds of thousands of years, we might find just the opposite. The earth's geographic poles are different from the magnetic poles. The geographic poles lie on the earth's axis, which is the imaginary line that the earth rotates around.

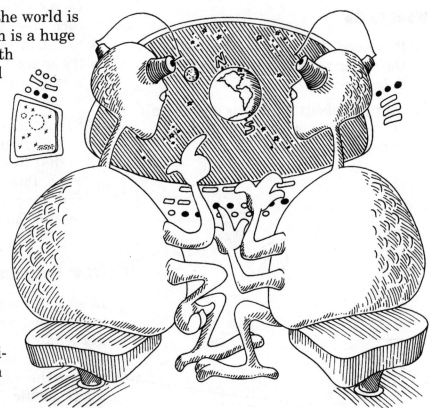

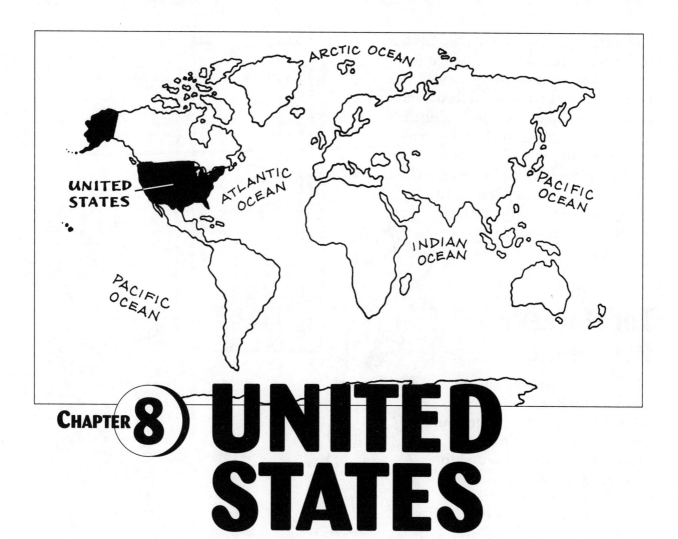

CHAPTER 8 UNITED STATES

Since its earliest beginnings, the United States has encouraged scientific discovery and invention. Scientists now come from all over the world to study and work in U.S. universities and laboratories. There have been more Nobel Prize–winning scientists from the United States than from any other country.

One area in which the United States has always excelled is space exploration. The United States landed the first man on the moon, Neil Armstrong, on July 21, 1969. The space shuttle program launched the first reusable spacecraft in 1981. The first female astronaut to fly in the space shuttle was Sally Ride, who flew in two different missions, the first in 1983 on the shuttle *Challenger*.

THE ROCKET'S RED GLARE

The space shuttle missions not only conduct important scientific research in space but also enable the world's most expensive repair personnel to do their work. Astronauts have fixed faulty satellites, realigned telescopes, and launched scientific instruments. Moving around in space can be tricky. Astronauts use a Manned Maneuvering Unit (MMU), which is like a backpack with rocket thrusters. The thrusters push the astronauts around by releasing compressed nitrogen gas. Here is a way of making your own rocket thrusters.

You Will Need

½-gallon (2-liter) plastic soda bottle, with top

large nail

hammer

2 straws (one must be wider than the other)

modeling clay

scissors

eraser (the pointed type that fits on the end of a pencil)

pencil

construction paper

glue

adult helper

What to Do

1. Have an adult poke a large hole through the top of the soda bottle using the hammer and nail. The hole should be large enough for the thinner straw to fit through.

2. Fit the thinner straw through the hole and seal around the edges with modeling clay.

3. Cut the fatter straw to a length of about 4 inches (10 cm) and place the eraser on one end of that straw.

4. Use the pattern here to trace four triangles on the construction paper. Cut out the triangles.

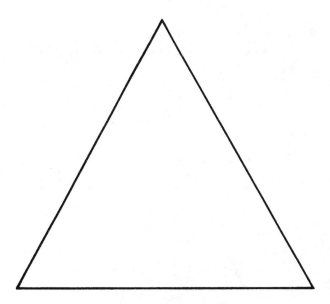

5. Glue the triangles to the larger straw on the end opposite to the eraser. The triangles should form the shape of tail fins (see diagram).

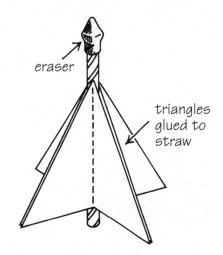

eraser

triangles glued to straw

6. Slide the thicker straw of the "rocket" over the thinner "launching" straw.

7. Hold the rocket so that it is not pointing at anything or anyone. Squeeze the bottle quickly to launch the rocket.

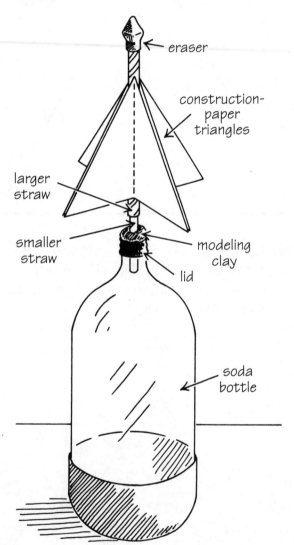

eraser

construction-paper triangles

larger straw

smaller straw

modeling clay

lid

soda bottle

What Happened

When you squeezed the bottle, you forced the air into an enclosed space. The air **compressed** (became squeezed together) in this space and created increased **pressure** (the amount of force acting in an area), which caused the "rocket" to launch, or blow off. The escaping air was under greater pressure than the air surrounding it. The rocket continued to be pushed forward until the pressure of the escaping air and the surrounding air became equal.

When a rocket blasts off, it blows off hot gases from the burning fuel. The gases from the fuel move in one direction, causing the rocket to go in the opposite direction. The important thing is not that the gases push against the ground or the air, but that they move away from the rocket. This is why rockets can operate in outer space where there is no air. The space shuttle uses large removable rockets for launching and smaller rockets to maneuver in space.

Orange You Glad?

The only scientist to win two Nobel Prizes independently was from the United States—Linus Pauling. He won the 1954 Nobel Prize for chemistry and the Nobel Peace Prize in 1962 for his opposition to the testing and use of nuclear arms. Linus Pauling also had strong views on the use of vitamin C to fight disease. He spent many years experimenting with the use of large doses of vitamin C to preserve health and prevent disease. Some of his ideas on this subject have not been well accepted by other scientists and doctors. Here is an experiment that allows you to see how much vitamin C is contained in some common beverages.

You Will Need

water

measuring cup

shallow bowl

aerosol spray starch (available at grocery stores)

tincture of iodine (available at drugstores)

measuring spoons

glass or jar

fresh orange juice

eyedropper

other juices

adult helper

What to Do

Caution: Do not eat or drink any of the chemicals used in this experiment.

1. Pour 1 cup (250 ml) of water into a shallow bowl.

2. Take the bowl outside. Hold the spray starch can about 6 inches (15 cm) above the top of the bowl of water and spray the starch into the bowl for 10 seconds.

1 cup (250 ml) water

shallow bowl

IODINE

3. Have an adult add ½ teaspoon (2 ml) of iodine to the water and stir. You will now have a blue test solution.

4. Place a tablespoon (15 ml) of the test solution in a glass or jar.

5. Use an eyedropper to add orange juice drop by drop to the test solution. Stir after each drop. Keep adding the orange juice until the blue color disappears. Count the number of drops of orange juice you used.

6. Try step 5 of this experiment again, this time using different kinds of juice.

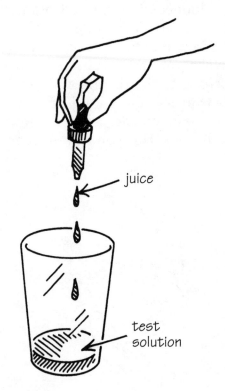

juice

test solution

What Happened

The vitamin C in the orange juice reacted with the iodine in the test solution. The starch and iodine together have a blue color. When all the iodine reacted with the vitamin C, the liquid became colorless.

Different juices contain different amounts of vitamin C. The more juice you need to add to get rid of the blue color, the less the vitamin C content of the juice. This is because each vitamin C particle reacts with an iodine particle. If you need more juice, that means there was not enough vitamin C to react with all the iodine.

CHAPTER 9 RUSSIA

Russian scientists have made many great discoveries
over the last 250 years. They have been world leaders in
space exploration, **astronomy** (space science), physics,
and chemistry. Chemist Karl Karlovich Klaus found an
element in 1844 that he called "ruthenium" (an old Latin
word for Russia). As far back as 1895, physicist Konstantin
Eduardovich Tsiolkovsky solved problems with rocket
travel. He was the first to suggest that rockets could use

liquid fuel to lift off. In 1954, Russia was the first country to build a nuclear reactor to generate power for cities and factories.

On June 29, 1995, Russian astronauts on the space station *Mir* welcomed aboard U.S. astronauts from the space shuttle *Atlantis* during the first ever docking with a U.S. space shuttle. The two crafts remained joined together for five days, during which time the astronauts conducted several research projects together.

And a recent Russian discovery may soon be on your shelves: Scientists in Niopik have created a new product that eliminates odors. They are hoping to sell it to companies in the United States.

Odor Eaters

What things do you not like to smell? Maybe it's that egg salad sandwich you left in your backpack. Or perhaps it's a piece of fish or moldy cheese in the back of the fridge. There's good news for you. Russian scientists have discovered that a material called phthalocyanine can get rid of 95 percent of bad odors! Traditional carbon (charcoal) filters can take away only about 5 percent of bad odors.

The Russian design uses this new material in special carbon filters to eliminate the nasty smell. Here's a way to examine how carbon filters work in removing dirt and some odors.

Warning: Do not taste or drink any of the water you have filtered.

You Will Need

large plastic soda bottle

scissors

paper coffee filter

charcoal briquettes (*not* with lighter fluid added)

paper bag

hammer

fine sand

several cups of muddy water

perfume

adult helper

What to Do

1. Have an adult help you cut the top third off of a plastic soda bottle. This will give you the container (the bottom piece) and a filter holder (the top piece with the cap removed).

2. Turn the "filter holder" upside down like a funnel and place it in the container. Open the coffee filter and place it in the holder.

3. Put the charcoal briquettes into the paper bag and place the paper bag on a hard outdoor surface (like a sidewalk). Hit the bag with a hammer to crush the briquettes.

4. Place a 1-inch (2.5-cm) layer of wet sand in the bottom of the filter. Add about the same amount of powdered charcoal on top of this layer. Add another layer of wet sand, then a final layer of powdered charcoal.

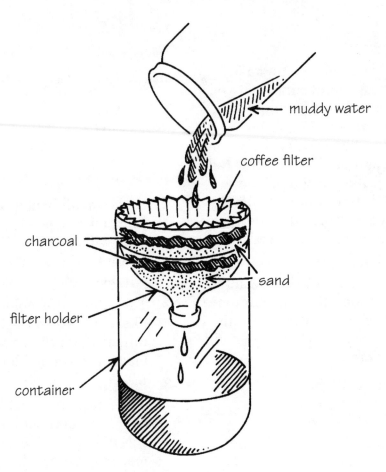

muddy water

coffee filter

charcoal

sand

filter holder

container

5. Add a drop of perfume to the muddy water. (Not too much—just enough so you can barely smell it.) Slowly pour the muddy water into the filter and allow it to drip through into the container. Be careful not to pour the water too quickly, as it will overflow the filter.

6. When all the water has dripped through into the container, remove the filter and set aside. What color is the water in the container? Does it still smell like perfume?

What Happened

The filter removed much of the dirt from the water and some of the odor. The filter had holes too small for the dirt to go through. The charcoal removed some of the smaller particles and most of the chemicals causing the odor because these materials **adsorbed** (became attached to the surface of a solid) onto the surface of the charcoal. Since the pieces of charcoal were too large to go through the filter, the adsorbed materials were trapped. The sand kept the charcoal particles from clumping up and stopping the flow of water through the filter.

AMAZING SCIENCE

Do you get hungry when you hear the noon-hour bell at your school? Does the sound of the bell remind you that it is time to eat? Russian scientist Ivan Pavlov experimented with this phenomenon. He discovered that if a dog were given food when a bell was rung, it would soon drool at the sound of a bell alone. This famous experiment—performed in 1902—was one of the first to explain how to control behavior.

CHAPTER 10 AUSTRALIA

Can you imagine playing on the beach at Christmastime, or throwing snowballs in July? Australia is sometimes called the "land down under" because it is below the equator. Its seasons are opposite to those found in countries above the equator. When it is winter in London or New York City, it is summer in Australian cities like Brisbane or Sydney.

Australia was the first country to warn people about the dangers of too much sun. The government was so concerned

about the number of people getting sick, it created a campaign to make the people aware of how they could prevent skin cancer. They told people to *slip* on a shirt, *slop* on sunscreen, and *slap* on a hat.

SLIP, SLOP, SLAP

Light coming to us from the sun is made up of waves. These waves are of different lengths, and we can see only some of them. Sunlight also includes ultraviolet (UV) light waves, which are too short for us to see. Researchers have found that these **ultraviolet rays** can cause skin cancer. To protect people from the harmful sunlight, scientists have developed sunscreens. The strength of these sunscreens is indicated by sun protection factor **(SPF)** numbers. Here's an experiment you can do to see how well different strengths of sunscreens work.

You Will Need

plastic wrap

scissors

photosensitive paper (e.g., SUNPRINT paper—
    available from many toy shops)

tape

sunscreens with different SPF numbers

What to Do

1. Cut a piece of plastic wrap slightly larger than the photosensitive paper. Make sure you do not expose the photosensitive paper to any bright light until step 4.

2. Cover the photosensitive paper with the plastic wrap and, if necessary, tape the wrap in place.

3. Use the different sunscreens to paint a design on top of the wrap. Label the SPF number of each sunscreen.

4. Place the photosensitive paper in bright sunlight, following the directions on the package for the length of time to keep the paper in the sun.

What Happened

The areas where there was no sunscreen became lighter colored, while the areas covered with sunscreen did not change color as much. The greater the SPF number, the less the color changed. The ultraviolet rays from the sun caused the chemicals in the paper to react. Sunscreen contains chemicals that do not allow the ultraviolet rays to get through. The higher the SPF number of the sunscreen the more protection you will get from the ultraviolet rays. This means that when you use sunscreen, you can stay out in the sun for longer periods of time because less of the sun's radiation can get through to you.

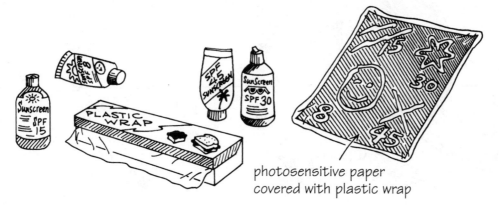

photosensitive paper
covered with plastic wrap

The Return of the Stick

Native to Australia are people known as **aborigines.** They arrived in the country about 40,000 years ago and lived as hunters and gatherers. When Europeans arrived in the country 200 years ago, there were about 1 million aborigines living there. Many of them died from the new diseases brought over from Europe, and many more died through fighting with the settlers. Today there are fewer than 200,000 of these people left.

The aborigines did not use guns or bows and arrows to hunt. Instead, they used a curved piece of wood called a **boomerang** to kill or knock down animals. The homemade boomerang you make in this experiment won't hurt anything, but it will come back to you.

You Will Need

two clean Styrofoam trays with curved ends, about 6 to 10 inches (15 to 25 cm) long (the kind used for packaging meat or poultry)

ruler

pencil or pen

scissors

glue or stapler

What to Do

1. Use a pen or pencil and a ruler to mark off two 1½-inch (4-cm) strips from the center of each Styrofoam tray. Carefully cut the tray along the lines. You now have 4 strips that are 6 to 10 inches (15 to 25 cm) long, with curved ends.

2. Glue or staple one pair of Styrofoam strips together in an X shape so that all the curved ends face downward. This will be your nonreturning boomerang.

3. Glue or staple the second pair of Styrofoam strips together in an X shape so that the curved ends of one strip face down and the curved ends of the other strip face up. This will be your returning boomerang.

STYROFOAM TRAY

1½ in. (4 cm)

1½ in. (4 cm)

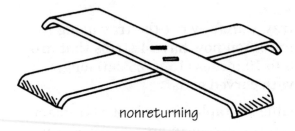

nonreturning

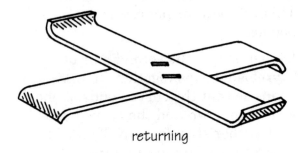

returning

What Happened

The boomerang from step 2 did not come back to you, but the boomerang from step 3 did. This is because of the way the boomerangs are shaped. When you throw a returning boomerang, the shape of the curved arms and the spinning of the boomerang cause the air flowing underneath it to lift one side and turn the boomerang. The shape of the arms of the nonreturning boomerang causes it to fly straight, cutting cleanly through the air.

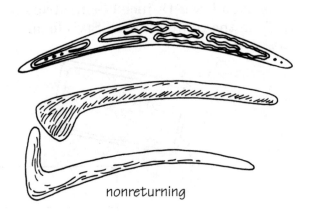

nonreturning

4. Hold the boomerang you made in step 2 by one of the arms. The curved ends should be facing upward. Use the same motion you normally would to throw a baseball overhanded. The boomerang should fly away from you in a downward chopping motion.

5. Do the same thing again, this time using the boomerang you made in step 3.

6. Try different methods of throwing the two boomerangs. Does the way they are thrown make any difference in their ability to return?

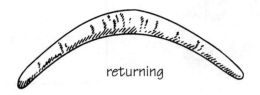

returning

Nonreturning boomerangs have quite sharp edges and are used for hunting. Returning boomerangs were originally used for hunting as well, but they are now used mostly for sport. Some returning boomerangs have been thrown as far as 100 yards (91 m) away and 150 feet (46 m) high and have still returned.

Did You Know

○ Boomerangs are not only from Australia. They have now been found on four other continents. The oldest boomerang was made from ivory and dates from 21,000 B.C. This boomerang was found in Poland in 1987.

GLOSSARY··

A

aborigines native group of people from Australia

adsorbed to become attached to the surface of a solid

air pressure the force that air places on a certain area

anchor a way of holding something firmly

archaeologists scientists who study the remains of past civilizations

astronomy space science

atoms the smallest particle of a substance that can be found using chemical methods

aviation the study of flight

B

bond to join together

boomerang curved piece of wood or bone

C

cable length of wire usually attached to an anchor

clepsydra a water clock

compressed to become squeezed together

crystals regularly shaped repeating units of chemicals

E

embalmed preserved bodies

engineers scientists who apply science and technology to solve practical problems

extinct no living examples left

F

fiber thin, threadlike pieces of plant or animal materials

force a push or pull

friction a force that resists motion when one surface slides over another

G

geologist a scientist who studies the Earth

gravity the force that pulls objects toward other large objects, such as the Earth

H

hieroglyphs a way of writing that uses pictures to represent a word, sound, or syllable

I

inclined plane sloped surface that allows you to raise objects to a higher level more easily

inertia a law of motion stating that objects which are not moving tend to stay in one place, while objects that are moving tend to stay moving in the same direction

insulin the drug that helps control diabetes

K

kerosene a liquid fuel made from coal

L

lard solid fat from animals

M

magnetic field lines of force around something that is magnetic

mass the amount of material something contains

mechanical advantage a number that represents the amount by which a machine multiplies the force used

molecule a small particle made up of two or more atoms

P

papyrus a type of reed used to make thin sheets to write on

penicillin a drug used to cure infections

pharaohs kings of Egypt

platform a flat, raised roadway

pressure the amount of force acting in a certain area

pyramid a four-sided tomb for pharaohs

R

refine take a material from its natural state and change it into another, more usable, form

S

seismic movement related to earthquakes

seismograph a device used to detect, measure, and record earthquakes

shaman tribal healer or religious leader

span the distance between towers on a bridge

SPF sun protection factor, or the protection factor in a sunscreen

standard time a system of time based on 24 time zones around the world

suspenders a device that holds something up

suspension bridge a bridge held up by cables

T

tectonic plates huge pieces of the earth's surface

tetrahedron a pyramid shape with four triangular faces

towers tall structures forming part of a bridge

tsunami a large ocean wave caused by an earthquake or volcano

U

ultraviolet rays a type of light ray that causes sunburn and skin damage

V

vacuum an empty space that contains no air

INDEX

embalmed, 4, 77
engineers, 18, 77
extinct, 39, 77

F

fibers, 10–12, 78
filters, 65–67
Fleming, Sir Sanford, 37
friction, 6, 31, 78

G

geologist, 38, 78
Germany, 23–27
Gesner, Abraham, 38–39
gravity, 30
Gutenberg, Johannes, 23–24

H

hieroglyphs, 18, 78
Hodgkin, Dorothy, 33, 35
hourglass, 13

I

inclined plane, 6, 78
inertia, 31,78

J

Japan, 47–54
June Bug, 42

K

kerosene, 39, 41, 78
kites, 42–44
Klaus, Karl Karlovich, 63

L

lard, 38, 78

M

magnetic field, 52–54, 78
Manned Maneuvering Unit, 56

towers, 19, 79
Ts'ai Lun, 10
Tsiolkovsky, Konstantin
    Eduardovich, 63
tsunami, 47, 48, 79

U

ultraviolet light, 70–71, 80
United Kingdom, 29–35
United States, 55–61, 64

V

vacuum, 25–26, 80

vitamin C, 59–61
von Guericke, Otto, 24–25

W

Wright Brothers, 42

Z

Zhang Heng, 10, 15–16
Zu Chonzhi, 10